WILTED ROSE PETALS OF DEAD LOVE

Brittany Riley

BookLeaf Publishing
India | USA | UK

Wilted rose petals of dead love © 2021

Brittany Riley

Presentation by BookLeaf Publishing

Web: www.bookleafpub.com

E-mail: info@bookleafpub.com

ISBN: 9789358361407

First edition 2021

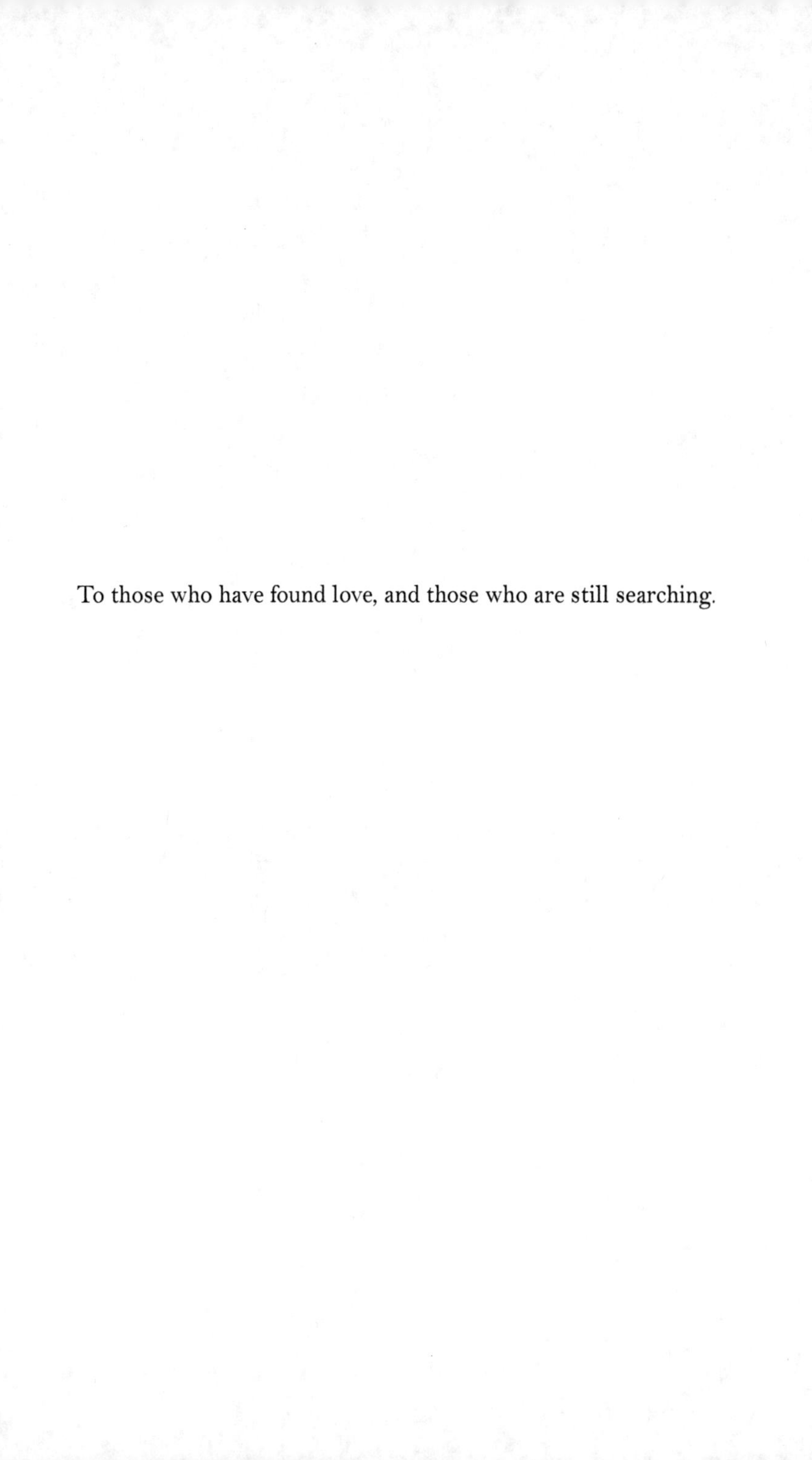

To those who have found love, and those who are still searching.

THE GENERAL ORDER OF THINGS...

absence/fonder, After, Age 6, black plum bauble, Blackheart, Carnivorous, Death (XIII), Foam, Goodbye, Grey, Hath, Juliet, Legacy, Lighthouse, Love note, Luminescence, Melancholy, My love for him is in roses, Second Love, Skin, Sunday, Teacup, Tempest, the human experience, The Singer, Vortex, White Lies, Wilted rose petals of dead love | 1984, Winter, Zombie

ABSENCE/FONDER

the blue asphyxiation of heart-break,
the bitter red pill of settling. choose.

which hurts less?
re memory as icy water droplets
      that trickle and recoil the spine
or dressed as a circus puppet, conditioned to tradition?
choose.

at night especially how his mind wanders and plays with
ghosts of she;
she with the gypsy heart and tinkling laughter of free-willed
angels, his mind dangles the good memories before the awful
ones for its own amusement
 he forgets butter menthols don't remove glass from hardwood
           floors
        dwelling gets you killed
          so leave
pack the moon in the trunk and slam it shut
with whiskey bottles

he'll bury it deep for peacemakers
to forage instead

AFTER

she wasn't afraid after, she was before, but not after

not scared of an outback sky so unfathomably big
unbothered by how it resembled a milky dam balanced on a
collapsible prayer
she stared a big black cloud straight in the eyes like a muted
beast and didn't blush with fear

      because
she reasoned
      how could it hurt when everything is already lost

she wasn't afraid after
of naked-eyed danger
she was before, but not after

she welcomes the clamorous killers
she isn't left to question a motive
      of diseased sweets

AGE 6

A sharp gasp cuts the little girl's laugh
upon seeing her divine token

A delicate pluck
from mother earth

Two hands and eyes scrunched like paper
an almighty breath escapes as a single blow

And so the silvery wisps fall
down

down

down

To their rebirth
as a silent prayer

For pink cake and white unicorns
and impish fairies with magical pixie dust

And all the things grown up eyes
can no longer see

BLACK PLUM BAUBLE

"you injure yourself"
***

because why would you crave the silken flesh
that poisons you
and makes you gasp for air after being stuck in the
oxygenless depths of ocean for eons
upon eons
upon eons
floating

"Ironclad, unbreakable"
***

he spews false promises and fables
to an iron mistress
heart of steel no longer glass
now anarchist bone
he made sure of that

his maiden's silver sword pierces silken flesh of the black
plum bauble
sweet the fruit but the inferno rages
squelches quivering muscle
of whipped butter and cotton clouds
and trickles the rouge human potion
until the red pools of suffrage drown them both

he'll say it was worth it

***

"they're finally free"

BLACKHEART

Coal eyes
assess bodies
like ghosts

Steel fingers
caress flesh
like rose petals

Dripping moans
escape lips
like molten honey

Tattoos vibrate
along buried veins
like turbulent rivers

Destroy my lips
as they crush yours
like painful desire

Don't stop
until I beg you
to continue

My demon saint
Blackheart

CARNIVOROUS

even the purest ivory hearts
      self-destruct
   in the blasphemy of heartbreak

red stains testify to annihilation
white fur of a polar bear's coat
      painted rouge in the shade, 'battle scars'
      CAUTION: WET PAINT

      the mirrored surface bears no resemblance
      of feeble innocence

merely child's play in Chernobyl

DEATH (XIII)

awaken beneath the surface some 10,000ft down
everything's a little blurry
     barnacles season the skin

no time no hiding no choice
to hedge one's bets
     swimming in shallow puddles

     drink the saline Adam's ale
          like O^2

     inhale cutlass suffrage
     exhale ivory doves
     *

     peace (a new life) awaits

FOAM - *INSPIRED BY "HYMN TO THE SEA"*

a trillion pools
of every blue
hue

shield her
glacial crux

> measly men
> appease
> h e r
> with jewels

> and supple flesh
> and wooden
> playthings

> left to rest

> on her bosom

as mortal offerings

left to rot

as mesmeric melodies

to lull her ire

the moaning tide endures

GOODBYE

i'm giving up on you,
and i'm not doing it lightly.

i just know i deserve better,
when i would have moved
mountains for you,

and you can't even collect feathers

for me.

GREY

How am I supposed to
move on

when

I see your chocolate eyes
in the dirt after it rains,
and in the mountain crevices
that echo
the darling shape of
your eyelids
as you laugh

when

your cradling touch,
has me drowning in rose petals
with no desire
for rescue

when

your absence
dwindles my sunshine,
and you watch
another man's uninspiring touch
leave me
glass half empty

when

you see me
choke
on tears,
with your name
inscribed on each
like trinkets

when

will you find
home again

when?

HATH

I carry my heart
in my purse.

Right beside the rouge lipstick
that will stain your
ivory collar,

the silver dagger
that will caress your bones
so gingerly,

and the needle and thread
that I will use
after returning it to you
as an offering,

in the palm of my outstretched hand.

JULIET

I knew love once. "The timing just wasn't right." "Maybe in the afterlife, things'll be different." And maybe we'll swim in the rivers of Atlantis, and it won't be blood that drowns us, it'll be piccolos of golden blossoms. You'll sip nectar from creases on my skin, play melodies on my bones, hush the silence in peace. The gods will envy how my eyes drink your essence and lap ecstasy in your embrace; mere immortals carried through galaxies as stars unbroken- as muses of Shakespeare and Aphrodite. Plastic negatives of you and her together won't incinerate my lungs with emerald flickers of unrequited devotion like it did when I was human. On this plane, and the next, it's impossible not to love you, my love. ~ You're mine.

LEGACY

If someday I'm not here, look for me...

in the trill of a music box,
in the rays of a full moon,
in the whip of a candle flame,
in the stone of castle walls,
in the pauses of poetry...

body and soul, I'll be there.

LIGHTHOUSE

Who saves the lighthouse
when it's weary?

A mothership
for the motherless

a thankless gallery to sea shanties
whipped to shore across choppy waters

beacon to starved ravens
and homesick men
ally to the sirens
and keeper of fables
faithful servant of the sun
and guidepost of helmsmanship

a slave with no master

who
saves
the saviour–
the orphan,
the homing pigeon,
condemned with the charter
of saving souls–
when it's weary?

A fruitless job. A faint-hearted task for the heartless. Loyal to
its duty.

Who saves the unbroken one, numbed to tenderness, so long
ago?

LOVE NOTE

You come home to me
to our home
and find me alone

I've had a hard day
My tears are caked
My heart is tired

All I wanted
In the darkest moments of the day
was you
and your touch
Your breath upon my skin
lingering warmth like tiny sparks
My own piece of home

So now
come to me
Hug me from behind
kiss beneath my ear
and buoy me in your embrace
Tell me you love me
and assure me everything is okay

I believe you when you say it
Tell me again
and again
Let's drift away from here

and lose ourselves
in deep seas

I know I'm safe
Your voice
your body
is my anchor

Don't you dare release me

LUMINESCENCE

hope is found
on

foggy leaves as lightbulbs
water droplets
as fluorescent globes
wildflowers as polka dots

and in the tender kiss of sunrise
when insomnia is your wintry captor

MELANCHOLY

she's got otherwordly rage
trapped in a human ribcage
      at one million degrees

flames lap at white bone, ashen
shrieking flesh, bubbles red

the tigress's wrath will not lull
so long as her mortal eyes
burdened with betrayal
      corrode to hollow pools

MY LOVE FOR HIM IS IN ROSES

My love for him is in roses

                    a layer of admiration
                     a layer of hatred
                      a layer of love
                         repeat

Until you reach the core

A dress in every colour
White for peace
Rouge for war

Don't come too close because I bite
Blood is his penance

My love for him is in roses
My beauty
may wilt
but he will remember me long after my petal skin is crushed to
dust beneath the soil
where I belong

SECOND LOVE

She was changing.
Vulnerable, hopeful, frightened,
foreign in a homely place.
Questions and answers, blurred emotions, searching and lost,
then,
a meet,
by chance, perhaps.
A breath, a pound, a touch of flesh,
her search suddenly fulfilled.
Captured moments of bliss,
an immortalization of the senses.
Time escaped through an hourglass,
safety and warmth encompassed her now.
She knew not of the future, nor what it held,
but she saw her future in his eyes.
Deep, turning, bonding,
she cannot have imagined it, please let it not be.
For her heart dances softly in hope,
like an autumn leaf drifting in search of safe landing.
She is fragile, as is he,
two wonderful pieces of whole.
She's patient with him,
dreaming, wishing, smiling,
continuing in the forest of her own dreams,
until her future arrives.

SKIN – *A HAIKU*

at dusk Gaia unveils
her intricate freckled organ
mistaken for stars

SUNDAY

She's grateful for little pockets of paradise.

daybreak kisses on naked cheeks
warmed by the kitchen window, doubled as a glass portrait.

fingertips in oversized sweaters.
more room for comfort
that way;
more room for her love

she adores the glint of sunrise
on darling wedding rings
as she reaches for
her coffee pot

and lulls in the soundscapes
of fairy wrens
dabbling as melodic artisans
on wintry railings

they're paid
with only the smiles they bring
to her

she: wife. mother. lover. and avid collector of paradise
pockets.

TEACUP

a regent clink
murmurs
as
crinkled fingertips
entwine
the neck
of a porcelain
  s
     w
   a
n

corrugated lips
and the leafy elixir
exchange silent contracts:
"a kiss
for a taste."

she obliges willingly

the tempered black liquid
more than sustenance
but an ode

to lineage
hand squeezes
milky storms
salted tears

among friends
and home

all cupped
into gold-tipped
fragile
porcelain
and shielded
behind glass

with the scent
of ancient forests

TEMPEST

Like a broken-hearted ocean
swallowing itself
in rage
and slamming its fingers
against unsuspecting shores

Until
there's nothing left
but the bones of wilful destruction
and an echo of immortal sorrow

THE HUMAN EXPERIENCE

they never questioned
immortality, as
a sparkling dot
of night haven

a speck in the cosmos
a drop in the ocean
just as v   a   s   t
as the last dusted granules of chemical complexity
whisper goodbye

cataclysmic consciousness
of a sapien heart
as it b u r n s
into oblivion

or rests
in an earthen sepulchre
as cyclic sustenance
for all eternity

nothing tangible is left

but the rotting flesh
of that biotic creature

with a mortal name

THE SINGER

Times like this

I think
of all
the seedy bars
in abandoned dungeons
where only spirits linger this late

Their broken souls
transpire
with broken dreams

Haunting trinkets of lullabies
that cut
bleeding hearts

Flooding rouge
trickles from the
corner stage
to the bar

where the floor
sighs

VORTEX

are you afraid of the dark
blanketing sunshine

or the rain as it pebbles upon glass?

translucent shadowed waterfalls
on human canvas

cooing
caressing

•••••

a gentle press
of fingertips
cool glass met

nothing but maps
of untold truths

and home
unfound

WHITE LIES

Happiness is a construct. A contractual agreement with peace.

"A glimpse is free, any longer you pay in oxygen."

There is no sunshine in pitiless depths of loathing. At failing your mission. At daring to tread where you brain warned you not to.

A few decades of lust isn't long enough. Barely enough time to understand someone when you don't know yourself. Not truly.

Dandelions.
Dead birds.
Dusted.

Nature doesn't fear the afterlife. It only fears humanity.

WILTED ROSE PETALS OF DEAD LOVE |

1984

Honey danced 'round her apartment drunk to the beat of his name
she hears it in every synth of a love ballad
for five minutes straight

      screams bastard
between rewinds of plastic cassettes and whiskey gulps

amazing how a tobacco haze adds pizzazz to Honey's tortured monologue
she finds herself a living breathing subject
of a horror movie of disconnect
in the deafening silence of the phone line
      but

her ears revel in the volume of everything else-
in melodies painting epic heartbreaks and wilful innocence of hearts now heinously tattooed
at the hands of lovers

      Honey's cold-blooded loneliness rises at dusk now;
almost vampiric

midnight is her one-night stand

WINTER

Glass tendrils
constrict the skin
of her neck,
where your lips
once promised
not to slice her open.

Her ribcage
fractures,
like a winters' leaf,
crushed to dust,
the moment someone utters
your name.

While she wanders
in darkness,
as the chilled air burns
her fragile chest,
barely mended
with spider's silk,
and the warm, wispy air,
clouding her lips,
the only proof she's alive.

And yet you prosper,
upon the molten skin of your
new lover.
Layers upon layers

of wool and cotton and feathers,
there to caress you,
and shield you from the cold,
where you abandoned her.

She's building castle walls
around the steel cage
you put her in,
where even the fiercest fire
cannot dissolve its frozen hold.

Not even a droplet,
not even a tear,
will be spared,
ever again.
Not again,
for you to destroy,
with your soul of a starved wolf,
disguised as a spring lamb.

ZOMBIE

when i say you broke my heart that day,
i don't mean that merely dropped it
like some inexpensive glass vase,
no.

you blew it into oblivion,
as my back turned
and I fell to my knees-
the collateral damage
in one of those silent movies

My body went to war that day

less than dust, not even the molecules survived
my soft, molten heart,
ready to love you
immortally muzzled
(a rabid beastly thing)

you just watched
as i bled out meagerly
with a gaping hole in my chest
where my naivety once rested

in the aftermath
alone
shell shock is an honourable seer

www.ingramcontent.com/pod-product-compliance
Lightning Source LLC
LaVergne TN
LVHW010833200726
843508LV00012B/2588